Legendary Warriors

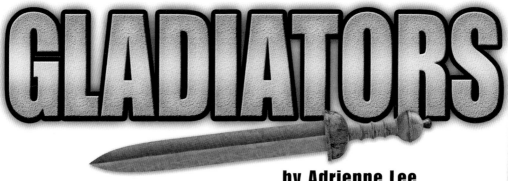

by Adrienne Lee

Consultant:
Barbara J. Fox
Professor Emerita
North Carolina State University

CAPSTONE PRESS
a capstone imprint

Blazers Books are published by Capstone Press,
1710 Roe Crest Drive, North Mankato, Minnesota 56003
www.capstonepub.com

Library of Congress Cataloging-in-Publication Data
Lee, Adrienne, 1981–
    Gladiators / by Adrienne Lee.
    pages cm. — (Blazers books. Legendary warriors.)
    Includes index.
    Summary: "Describes the lives of Gladiator warriors, including their training, weapons,
and fighting techniques"—Provided by publisher.
  ISBN 978-1-4765-3114-4 (library binding)
  ISBN 978-1-4765-3372-8 (ebook pdf)
  1. Gladiators—Juvenile literature. I. Title.
GV35.L44 2014
796.80937—dc23   2013010313

Editorial Credits
Megan Peterson and Mandy Robbins, editors; Kyle Grenz, designer; Wanda Winch, media
researcher; Jennifer Walker, production specialist

Photo Credits
The Bridgeman Art Library/© Look and Learn/Private Collection/Angus McBride, 23, ©
Look and Learn/Private Collection/Harry Green, 25; Capstone: Chris Forsey, 26; Corbis:
Bettmann, 6, 17, 20, Heritage Images, 8-9; Courtesy of Miles Kelly Publishing: Mike White,
13; Dreamstime: Philcold, 29; fotolia: xavier, cover (gladiator); Getty Images Inc: DEA/L.
Romano, 11; Newscom: akg-images, 27, akg-images/Peter Connolly, 14-15, Design Pics/
George Munday, 5; Shutterstock: bigredlynx, back cover (sword), greglith, cover (bottom),
Matab, cover (background), nito, 19, Pavel L. Photo and Video, 28

Printed in the United States of America in Stevens Point, Wisconsin.
032013   007227WZF13

Table of Contents

ANCIENT ROME

Long ago, the gladiators of Rome fought bloody battles for the enjoyment of others. These well-trained warriors fought in stadiums called **amphitheaters**. Most Romans enjoyed watching the deadly battles.

From about 500 BC until AD 500, Rome was the biggest and most important city in the world.

amphitheater—a large, open-air building with rows of seats in a high circle around an arena

The Romans made slaves of soldiers they defeated. Slaves could buy their freedom, but the price was high. Only slaves who were gladiators could earn enough money.

IT'S A FACT

A man called a lanista bought slaves and trained them to be gladiators.

In 264 BC, a man named Decimus Junius Brutus made three pairs of slaves fight to the death. This match was the first recorded gladiator contest.

Fights between gladiators were called games. Gladiator games were held in honor of the emperor. To start the games, gladiators entered the arena wearing purple cloaks.

emperor—a male ruler of a country or group of countries

arena—a large area that is used for sports or entertainment

The fighting between gladiators did not bother most Romans. The battles were considered a celebration of the values that made Rome great.

value—a belief or idea that is important to a person or people

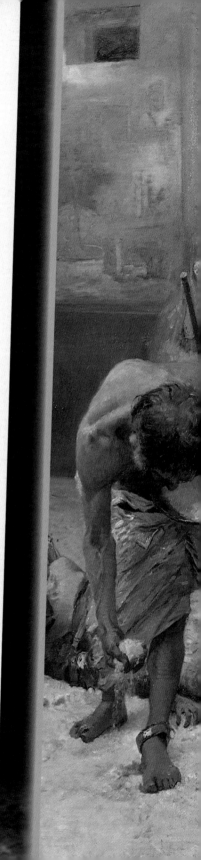

Those upset by the gladiator fights were thought to be weak.

LIFE AS A GLADIATOR

Gladiators trained in special schools. They had excellent trainers and the best medical care. Gladiators practiced using spears, daggers, and swords. They lifted weights to become stronger.

IT'S A FACT

A few free Roman citizens volunteered to be gladiators. These volunteers could leave the school. Slaves could not.

dagger—a short knifelike weapon with a sharpened surface on both sides

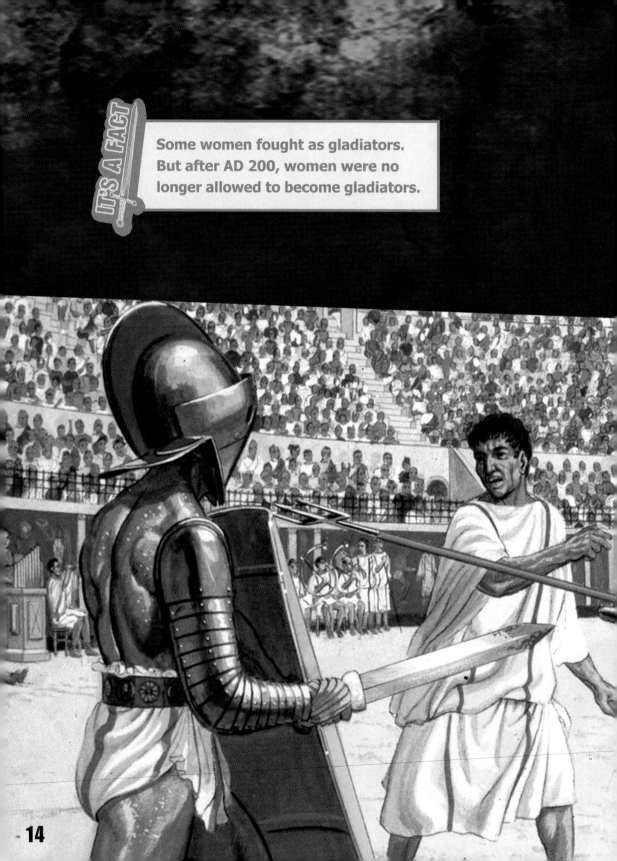

Some women fought as gladiators. But after AD 200, women were no longer allowed to become gladiators.

Gladiators fought two or three times a year. Not every match ended in death. Referees stopped matches if there was no clear winner.

To admit defeat, a gladiator threw down his shield and held up a finger. A "thumbs down" sign from the crowd meant he could live. But a "thumbs up" sign meant the winner must kill the loser.

IT'S A FACT

A very successful gladiator might be given a wooden sword called a rudis. It meant he was a free man.

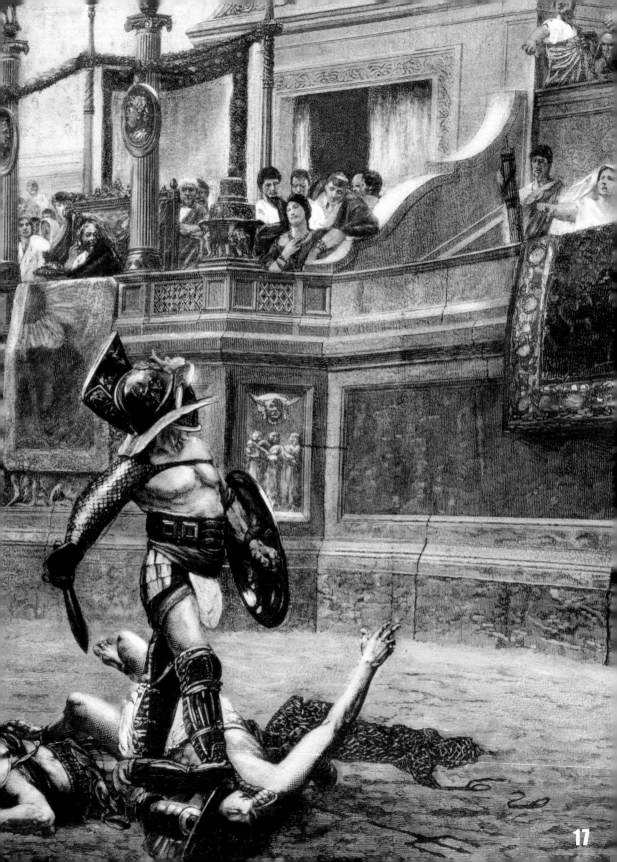

WAYS OF ATTACK AND DEFENSE

Gladiators fought with many weapons. A gladiator called a samnite fought with a sword and large shield. He also wore a helmet with a crest.

The first gladiators used a straight sword called a gladius. This weapon's name led people to call the fighters gladiators.

crest—a large ridge on the top of a helmet

samnite ➡

Some emperors chose to fight as gladiators. Gladiators who fought Emperor Commodus had to use wooden swords. Meanwhile, Emperor Commodus used a real sword.

A retiarius gladiator wore armor only on his left arm. He carried a net and a long spear called a **trident**. A retiarius trapped the other gladiator in his net. Then he stabbed him with his trident.

trident—a long spear with three sharp points at its end

Spartacus is history's most famous gladiator. In 73 BC, he helped 70 other gladiators escape a training school. Thousands of slaves joined him to form an army.

Spartacus' army defeated the Roman army many times before Spartacus was killed in battle.

THE END OF THE GLADIATORS

Gladiator games became most popular after AD 80. That year, a huge building known as the Colosseum opened in Rome. It held up to 50,000 people.

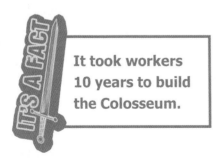

IT'S A FACT

It took workers 10 years to build the Colosseum.

In AD 306, Constantine the Great became Rome's first **Christian** emperor. Constantine spoke out against the bloodshed in the arena. Still, many Romans continued to watch the games.

Christian—a person who follows a religion based on the teachings of Jesus Christ

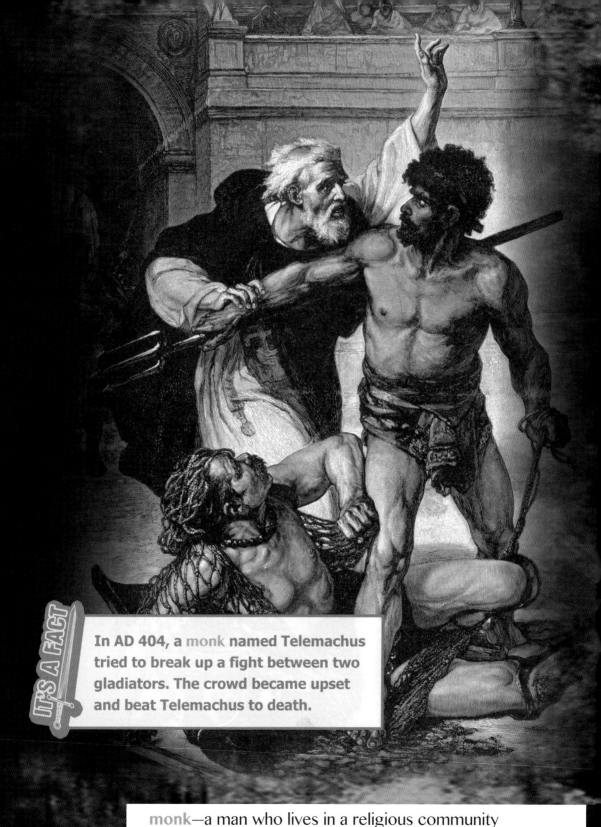

In AD 404, a monk named Telemachus tried to break up a fight between two gladiators. The crowd became upset and beat Telemachus to death.

monk—a man who lives in a religious community and promises to devote his life to his religion

⬆ **Today tourists visit the Colosseum in Rome.**

As more Romans became Christians, their values changed. The gladiator games officially ended in AD 440. Today people continue to visit Rome's Colosseum. They learn about what life was like for the gladiators.

GLOSSARY

amphitheater (AM-fuh-thee-uh-tuhr)—a large, open-air building with rows of seats in a high circle around an arena; in ancient Roman times, gladiators often fought in amphitheaters

arena (uh-REE-nuh)—a large area used for sports or entertainment

Christian (KRIS-chuhn)—a person who follows a religion based on the teachings of Jesus Christ

crest (KREST)—a large ridge on the top of a helmet

dagger (DAG-ur)—a short knifelike weapon with a sharpened surface on both sides

emperor (EM-puhr-uhr)—a male ruler of a country or group of countries

lanista (lah-NISS-tuh)—a person who owned and trained gladiators

monk (MUHNGK)—a man who lives in a religious community and promises to devote his life to his religion

trident (TRY-dent)—a long spear with three sharp points at its end

value (VAL-yoo)—beliefs or ideas that are important to a person or people

READ MORE

Guillain, Charlotte. *Gladiators and Roman Soldiers.* Fierce Fighters. Chicago: Raintree, 2010.

Park, Louise. *Blood in the Arena: Gladiators of Ancient Rome.* Ancient Civilizations. New York: PowerKids Press, 2013.

Roemhildt, Mark. *Gladiators.* History's Greatest Warriors. Minneapolis: Bellwether Media, 2012.

INTERNET SITES

FactHound offers a safe, fun way to find Internet sites related to this book. All of the sites on FactHound have been researched by our staff.

Here's all you do:

Visit *www.facthound.com*

Type in this code: 9781476531144

Super-cool stuff!

Check out projects, games and lots more at
www.capstonekids.com

INDEX